BEHIND
THE
LEGEND

If you purchased this book without a cover, you should be aware that this book is stolen property. It was reported as "unsold and destroyed" to the publisher, and neither the author nor the publisher has received any payment for this "stripped book."

 little bee books

An imprint of Bonnier Publishing USA

251 Park Avenue South, New York, NY 10010

Copyright © 2017 by Bonnier Publishing USA

All rights reserved, including the right of reproduction in whole or in part in any form.

LITTLE BEE BOOKS is a trademark of Bonnier Publishing USA, and associated

colophon is a trademark of Bonnier Publishing USA.

Manufactured in the United States LB 0317

Library of Congress Cataloging-in-Publication Data
Names: Peabody, Erin, author. | Rivas, Victor, illustrator.
Title: Bigfoot / by Erin Peabody; illustrated by Victor Rivas.
Description: First edition. | New York: Little Bee, [2017] | Series:
Behind the legend; 2 | Audience: Ages 8–10. | Audience: Grades 4 to 6.
Includes bibliographical references. | Identifiers: LCCN 2016040176 |Subjects: LCSH:
Sasquatch—Juvenile literature. | Monsters—Juvenile literature. | Curiosities and wonders—
Juvenile literature. | Classification: LCC QL89.2.S2 P43 2017 | DDC 001.944—dc23
LC record available at https://lccn.loc.gov/2016040176

First Edition 10 9 8 7 6 5 4 3 2 1

ISBN: 978-1-4998-0425-6 (pbk);

978-1-4998-0426-3 (hc)

littlebeebooks.com
bonnierpublishingusa.com

BIGFOOT

by Erin Peabody

art by Victor Rivas

little bee books

CONTENTS

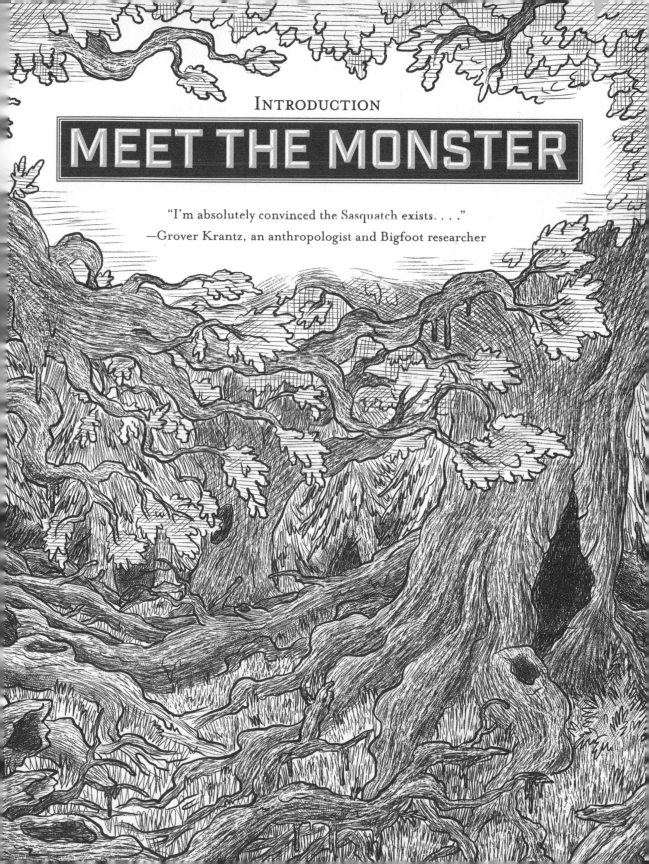

INTRODUCTION

MEET THE MONSTER

"I'm absolutely convinced the Sasquatch exists. . . ."
—Grover Krantz, an anthropologist and Bigfoot researcher

I magine that you're wandering through the woods with friends. Straight ahead, something catches your eye: the largest footprint you've ever seen! Trembling, you gently place your foot inside the eerie depression. It's *much* bigger than your own.

Others insist that they've heard Bigfoot. They've been jolted out of their sleep by strange howls, moans, knocks, and screams. Panicked by such disturbing sounds, witnesses have rushed to lock doors. They've been stunned to watch as their house pets—apparently spooked as well—refuse to go out into the dark night. How about you? Have you ever heard a strange rapping outside your bedroom window? Or come across unusual animal tracks in your yard?

Such gripping experiences have haunted some people their whole lives, including a few individuals you'll learn about in this book. Unfortunately, some of these folks died before ever learning for certain if Bigfoot really exists. What about us? Can we get a clean answer to this hairy question?

We can certainly try, thanks to the work of many curious investigators whose findings can help guide us. But before we head to the woods in search of the Big (and often smelly) Guy, let's first stomp back centuries ago to where our fascination with *big* began.

CHAPTER ONE
GIANT LEGENDS

"Fee-fi-fo-fum, I smell the blood of an Englishman!"
—The giant from *Jack and the Beanstalk*

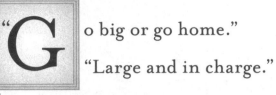

"**G**o big or go home."

"Large and in charge."

"Bigger is better."

Why are we obsessed with the oversized? Where did this fascination with all things colossal come from?

Well, it didn't start with us. We can blame at least part of this preoccupation on our ancestors, those ancient storytellers and mythmakers who dreamed up all sorts of large, as well as hairy, smelly, and even flatulent, humanlike beasts!

You've likely heard of some of them.
There's the one-eyed Cyclops from
Greek myths, a cave-dwelling loner
who is attacked for being too boorish,
brutish, and, well, too big. There's
also the giant of "fee-fi-fo-fum"
fame from the fairy tale *Jack and the
Beanstalk*, whom the penniless young
Jack manages to outwit.

Big evokes strength and power. It can also symbolize rebels and fighters, as in the Giants (or Gigantes) of Greek mythology who challenged the all-powerful gods but failed. And as the *Jack and the Beanstalk* tale reminds us, many giants also have a hearty appetite for humans. Technically, though, in the annals of fairy tales, giants who devour people are known as ogres. (Shrek has worked hard to improve this image!)

And it's not just male giants who get a hankering for humans. There are ogresses, too. In Japanese folklore, for instance, the ogress Onibaba, in her desperation to protect a child, is driven to nibbling on human flesh.

MODERN-DAY MONSTER?

Given this rich history of supersized beasts, it makes sense then that our generation of monster lovers has made room for another. And it needs a *lot* of room! The estimated eight-foot-tall, roughly eight-hundred-pound hairy stomper we're talking about, of course, is Bigfoot.

Some people are convinced that bigfoot-like creatures roam the giant fern forests of America's Pacific Northwest. This damp and lush region, also known for its skyscraping evergreen trees, includes parts of Alaska, Washington, Oregon, and California. According to some witnesses, the whole United States constitutes one big stomping ground for Bigfoot and his hairy cousins. Sightings are scattered across almost all of the fifty United States—and the world!

Hairy, wild men have played a role in many old and cherished Native American legends—proof, say believers, that bigfoots exist. For instance, the Quinault Indians of coastal Washington used to speak of a Bigfoot-like dinner robber known as "Glue-Keek." With glowing eyes and legs as large as tree trunks, this monster was said to terrorize women who worked in the berry patches, chasing them and crushing their

precious harvest as he went. Other tribes revered what they considered to be the big forest spirit, or "Oh-mah" ("Boss of the Woods"), as the Hoopa tribe of Northern California called him. And, of course, most everyone is familiar with Bigfoot's most popular alias, "Sasquatch." The name comes from the Salish people, whose tribes have lived for centuries on the coastlines of the Pacific Northwest and Canada.

HUSH, HUSH! DON'T CRY

Fairy tales containing bogeymen and monsters are popular around the world. For children living in the mountains of Asia—in places like Tibet and Nepal (where Mount Everest is located)—that fearful creature is the Yeti, aka the Abominable Snowman.

Lurking in the snow, the furry beast is said to chase after disobedient and unruly tots. Their only chance of survival is to run madly down the hill, hoping that the Yeti's grungy locks of hair will tumble into his eyes, rendering him blind and unable to catch them.

The Yeti tale was a real fright, according to a man who knew Everest better than anyone. Sherpa Tenzing Norgay, who famously helped Sir Edmund Hillary summit Everest in 1953, once recalled hearing frightening stories about the Yeti as a child. "Even to this day," he said, "you will find a naughty child hushed to silence when his mother says to him, 'Hush, hush, here comes the Yeti.'"

TALES FROM THE CRYPT

We generally recognize giants as make-believe, mythical bullies. They exist only in our minds (which can be frightening enough). But what about bigfoots? Their status, you might say, is a little fuzzier. Some people swear such creatures exist—insisting that they've seen one, heard one . . . even smelled one. But without concrete evidence, scientists cannot yet confirm this.

There's a name for these phantom biological misfits, which have not been officially documented: cryptids. Bigfoot and his many aliases fall within this group, which includes Sasquatch (linked mostly to Canada and the Pacific Northwest), Yowie (from the

Sasquatch

Yowie

Yeti

Land Down Under, Australia), and the Yeti (aka the Abominable Snowman), a white woolly beast from the Himalayas that can allegedly scale Everest better than any seasoned mountaineer!

Other cryptids seem to be ripped right out of a horror film. There's the Batsquatch (think Bigfoot with a bat head!), and the Bunyip, an Australian water beast featured in bedtime stories and said to gobble up children. (Sweet dreams, kids!) Another is the Wendigo, a terrifying zombie-like giant from Canada with sunken eyes and bloody lips.

Batsquatch

Bunyip

Wendigo

IT'S ALIVE!

Of course, no scientist really takes these grisly characters seriously. However, there have been a few cryptids across history that demanded a second look.

One of the most stunning discoveries was a fish, the coelacanth (SEEL-uh-kanth), which was thought to have died out more than sixty-five million years ago with the dinosaurs. But in 1938, a museum curator named Marjorie Courtenay-Latimer, with the help of a fisherman, discovered the primitive-looking fish (which can weigh up to two hundred pounds!) among his catch. As is customary in science, the creature was named after its finder. Thanks, Ms. Courtenay-Latimer, for giving us *Latimeria,* the genus of giant fishes!

Bigfoot isn't the only hairy, apelike cryptid that's listed in books on myths and legends. It turns out that one of East Africa's most beloved mammals, the mountain gorilla, was once thought to be a bloodthirsty brute capable of kidnapping—and eating—humans! (And we're supposed to be the smarter species?) Misunderstood for centuries, this generally shy forest lounger and leaf-eater was officially named in 1902 by a German explorer who relied on local African guides and well-worn

elephant trails to find his way into the gorillas' lush mountain habitat.

Armed with more knowledge now, most of us greatly admire the magnificent gorilla, a fascinating creature with which we share a large amount of DNA. Unfortunately, a lack of education about them still threatens these animals, which are critically endangered due to continued poaching and habitat destruction.

BIGFOOT, FUR REAL?

So what about the most famous of cryptids, the bigfoot? Could there be any scrap of truth to the wild tales that have been whispered 'round crackling campfires for the last sixty years? Such stories tell of a stinking beast that can hypnotize its victims, howl, and hurl rocks, yet also one that reminds us strangely of ourselves—with its humanlike footprints, fingers, and thumbs.

No doubt this shaggy eight-footer is part of our culture, whether you envision him as a cuddly Chewbacca-like beast or a misunderstood reject living on the fringes of society. But the questions we'll tackle in this book are: Do bigfoot-type animals really exist in nature? And what kind of evidence is there to prove this?

Like any good investigation, our quest for the truth must be guided by things we can see, hear, and touch. No matter how tempting it is to find evidence for bigfoots in Native American stories or in other ancient legends and tales (like those we've discussed earlier), we must rely on hard evidence for answers about these beasts. It's also disrespectful and foolish to assume that we know the meaning behind another culture's stories or legends.

So, let's begin. We'll start with a pivotal case in bigfoot history. The year was 1955 and a man, William Roe, was hiking in the mountains of British Columbia, Canada.

Suddenly, he came upon a stunning sight: a large creature that he later described as part animal, part man. It was nearly covered in silver-tipped, dark brown hair, and it sported long arms that nearly reached its knees from a standing position.

Then, he saw the creature start to walk, lifting its wide, heavy feet, directly toward him.

Chapter Two

BIGFOOT'S BEGINNING

"It was covered with hair. . . . It looked eight or ten
feet tall to me." —One of the first eyewitnesses who,
in 1958, claimed to see a bigfoot

William Roe, a highway worker out on a short break, was dumbfounded by what he saw. He searched his mind for explanations. He wondered: Is someone filming a movie in these woods? Is this creature really a person dressed in a costume?

Roe now stood within twenty feet of the animal. He watched as it grabbed at nearby branches, stripping them clean with its white teeth. The apelike creature then looked directly at him, with a facial expression that Roe could only describe as "amazement."

Eventually, Roe guessed, the beast caught a whiff of his scent and started to walk away. With one final glimpse, the apelike creature looked back over its shoulder at the man. And then, it was gone.

A FAMILY AFFAIR

But it wasn't gone for long. Having heard Roe's account, a few more individuals stepped forward, less hesitant and fearful about sharing their own hairy-man encounters. One was Albert Ostman, a retired logger, who claimed that decades earlier he had seen not just one bigfoot-like beast (He called it a sasquatch)—but an entire family of them!

As his story goes, Ostman was in British Columbia, Canada, in the 1920s, hunting for gold, when he was jerked awake one night from sleep—literally. He quickly realized that he was being carried, sleeping bag and all, through the woods by a sasquatch! After several hours, he said, the creature finally dropped him in a remote valley where the rest of the beast's hairy relatives lived. The sasquatch's family included an adult female (the mother) and two offspring, a young male and young female.

And there was more to Ostman's outrageous-sounding story. He related how the family of sasquatches communicated in grunts and how the young male even liked to scoot around on his bottom! Despite how ridiculous it all sounded, Ostman—just like Roe—signed a sworn statement, also known as an affidavit, that he was telling the truth. Even more, a local newspaper ran the story. Readers were captivated by the weird and wacky account, eager to believe a story that was never verified.

BIGFOOT IS BORN

A few years after William Roe's gripping account of watching a sasquatch munching on leaves in the Canadian woods, another sensational story surfaced. This one took place in California, and ultimately catapulted the whole region—and then the entire country—into bigfoot mania.

It was a typical workday in the summer of 1958 for Jerry Crew. Crew was a bulldozer operator at a logging company working in Bluff Creek, a wilderness area teeming with soaring spruce and other conifer trees in Northern California. Once he got to the work site, Crew traded his comfortable moccasins for his work boots, put on his hard hat, and strode over to his tractor. That's when he saw them: the largest, most deeply set footprints that he'd ever seen.

Climbing onto the tractor for a better look, the sight seemed even more staggering. Spread out before him on the freshly scraped earth was a series of large manlike footprints. They seemed so real, given their detail and deep impressions. But Crew figured it had to be a joke, likely one of the

fellas just pulling his leg. The men liked pulling pranks on one another; it helped the workweek pass more quickly.

And yet, Crew couldn't shake the image of the tracks from his head. He needed to tell the foreman about his discovery.

HOWLS OF LAUGHTER, OR FRIGHT, IN THE WOODS?

Were the whopping tracks that Jerry Crew discovered the product of a big hoax—or made by a real, hulking beast?

Tales and legends, as we discussed earlier, are an important part of people's culture. This is true, too, for the groups of men who historically worked in America's woods as hunters, trappers, and lumberjacks. (Sorry, ladies—women were denied access to these jobs until around World War II!) Just like the mountain men who roamed the Rocky Mountains in the mid-1800s, woodsmen would swap amusing and far-fetched tales to bide their time during long forays into remote forests.

One yarn told about mosquitoes that were so big, they could suck a cow dry. Another featured the Hodag, a totally mixed-up mythical beast that was said to possess a frog's face, a wide mouth full of razor-sharp teeth, and an arched back studded with stegosaurus-like plates!

According to one of the silliest yarns, even squirrels could be sinister. If an axman went to bed and found bits of rolled-up lichen in his sleeping bed, it was considered a threatening omen: the work of wicked Will-am-alones, squirrel-like rodents whose lichen stashes were said to cause terrifying nightmares!

HAIR-RAISING EPISODES

Wilbur "Shorty" Wallace, the man in charge, was hardly surprised when Crew told him about the footprints. Apparently, this wasn't the first time that large mysterious tracks had turned up at company worksites. The eerie prints had been noted at other locations, too. In addition, a string of unsettling incidents had recently transpired at the work site. A four-hundred-fifty-pound drum of gasoline had gone missing. A seven-hundred-pound tire had been mysteriously rolled into a ditch.

Shorty originally thought vandals were responsible for the hijinks, but now as he, Crew, and the other men talked, he wondered aloud if someone else—or something else—was responsible for the mischief. In the meantime, the men were certain of one thing: their name for the large-footed trespasser, "Bigfoot."

The comments and stories swirling about a bigfoot in the little Northern California community grew more unnerving. When four dogs went missing, people assumed it was the beast that snatched them . . . possibly to eat. Fresh footprints at work sites continued to appear. Many of the men at the logging company reported a strange, nagging feeling that they were being watched.

LOOKING FOR CLUES

Anxious for more answers, Crew traded his hard hat for a detective one (though not really)! He traced one of the large footprints he'd found onto paper. He learned how to create plaster casts by pouring wet, milky plaster into a print and waiting for it to harden and assume the shape of the track. One such track measured sixteen inches long!

Shorty's brother, Ray Wallace, another manager at the company, measured the beast's stride. At a regular pace, the bigfoot's prints were fifty inches apart; at a run, they measured ten feet apart!

It didn't take long before the buzz reached the news desk of a reporter at the local paper, California's *Humboldt Times*. In his story about the alleged bigfoot, the writer laid out the known facts about the alleged creature and then posed these questions to readers: Are the tracks a hoax? Or were the tracks a sign of "a huge but harmless wild-man, traveling through the wilderness?"

The Humboldt Times

VOLUME CXXV   NUMBER 1   THE HUMBOLDT TIMES, EUREKA, CALIFORNIA, SUNDAY, APRIL , 1958

GIANT FOOTPRINTS PUZZLE RESIDENTS ALONG TRINITY RIVER

The story ran on a Sunday. By Monday, reporters from several major U.S. newspapers, including the *New York Times* and *Los Angeles Times*, were pounding on the small California paper's doors.

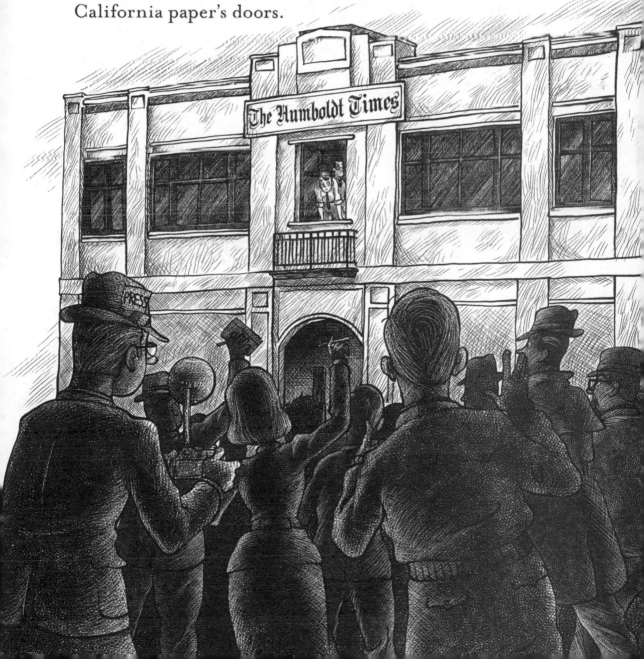

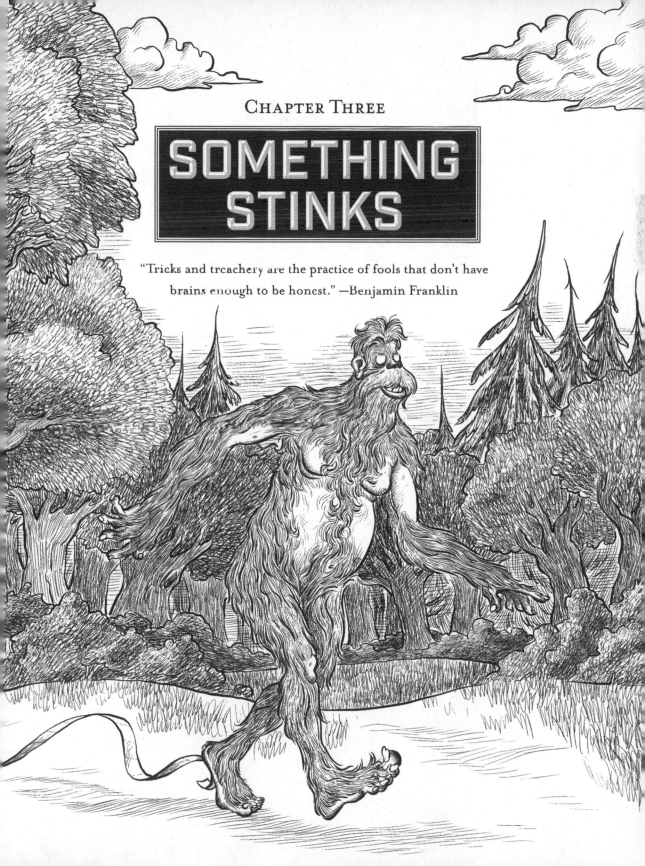

CHAPTER THREE

SOMETHING STINKS

"Tricks and treachery are the practice of fools that don't have brains enough to be honest." —Benjamin Franklin

Not everyone in Bluff Creek, California, was fearful or even humored by the news coverage of a possible wild man stomping around town. Skeptics shook their heads at what they considered total nonsense. To them, the fabulously large tracks had a familiar stench, one that traced back to a proven prankster: Ray Wallace. Wallace was one of the owners of the logging company, and he had a reputation for spinning colorful tales and playing practical jokes.

In fact, at one point during the Bigfoot saga in Bluff Creek, Wallace seemed so desperate for attention that he claimed to have captured a real

live sasquatch. Not only that, according to the logging company owner, the bigfoot was bonkers about cereal and would only eat hundred-pound bags of Kellogg's Frosted Flakes! Then, when researchers and others asked about seeing the hairy wonder, Wallace said the beast could be bought . . . for a modest one million dollars!

Increasingly, Ray Wallace looked suspect. He had a history of pranking, an apparent hunger for fame and money, and unique access to the "crime scene" (the site of the original Bigfoot tracks). If that weren't enough, the final nail in the coffin was delivered a few decades later. In 2002, the year Wallace died, his family revealed the *real* source of the tracks: a set of large, wearable wooden feet that belonged to the prankster!

It seemed that Wallace, along with his brother, Shorty, had wanted so badly to make it *big* that they were willing to fool thousands of people for decades.

But hoaxes and pranks didn't slake the public's interest in Bigfoot and bigfoot creatures. In nearby Willow Creek, part of the same mountainous region in northwestern California as Bluff Creek, citizens kicked off an annual tradition in honor

of the hairy hiker: Bigfoot Days. The weekend festival is still popular today and features a lot of Bigfoot-inspired music, food, souvenirs, and plenty of locals soberly warning tourists *not* to go in the woods.

The hunt for Bigfoot continued in earnest, too. Specially trained tracking dogs, including a German shepherd named White Lady, were enlisted in the search. Biologists from nearby universities were asked to examine mysterious tracks and consider what kind of creature could have made them. A psychic even tried to connect with Bigfoot telepathically!

CAUGHT—IN PICTURES

However, in all these searches, nothing turned up, nor was anything proven. But then, in 1967, the tide turned dramatically for Bigfoot enthusiasts. A pair of amateurs announced that they'd clinched the ultimate in terms of evidence: It was a sasquatch himself—actually, *herself*!—practically posing for the camera!

It happened this way: Two men with a love of the hairy hiker, Roger Patterson and Bob Gimlin, traveled to the Bluff Creek region to search for the beast's now-famous tracks. On a sunny day that autumn, they took their horses out to explore nearby creek beds and canyons, hoping to catch a bigfoot. And that, they said, they promptly did.

The horses alerted them first. The animals,
said Gimlin later, "started jumping around,
raising the devil. . . ." In all the excitement,
Patterson's horse tossed him to the ground. The
cause of the spooking soon became clear. It was a
creature standing by a creek, about one hundred
twenty-five yards away. It had a humanlike head

that bore a large forehead and wide nostrils. Dark thick hair covered most of its body. Its arms hung almost to its knees.

And all of this, Patterson managed to capture on videotape. The result is a shaky and grainy one-minute video that you can find online—with your parents' permission, of course.

BEASTIE BOY, OR GIRL?

The creature's other curious features were, well
. . . its breasts. Bigfoot, at least this specimen,
was very much a female! And it didn't dart off
immediately. According to Patterson, the creature
seemed relaxed, as if it "had seen people before."

In the last sequence, the She-Squatch looks
back over her shoulder at the two men. It was a
familiar gesture, that sideways gaze. Hadn't it been
described by some other observer before?

By that time, the men had run out of film, having wasted much of it, they said, filming autumn leaves. And they tried pursuing the creature, but they became too rattled to do so, fearing the protective mother (if that's what she was) had babies or youngsters nearby.

But it hardly mattered. The two hunters had what they wanted—proof, caught on film, that bigfoots were real. Other Bigfoot enthusiasts were gleeful, too, declaring that the decades-long investigation into hairy, apelike creatures was now closed. "We had the film," remarked a leading Bigfooter. "We thought it was all over."

FREEZE-FRAME

However, it was just the beginning. Over the course of the next several months and years (going on fifty now), the Patterson–Gimlin film has been watched more times than any viral YouTube video.

It's also been analyzed, frame by frame, to see what additional information the footage might tell us. Animation experts have applied their skills and so have special-effects specialists from Hollywood. Yet there remains no overwhelming consensus on whether the video features a hairy marvel of nature . . . or simply a person in a gorilla suit.

WALK THIS WAY

Some of the most helpful critiques have been offered by anthropologists—scientists who study how humans develop over time. Specifically, some of these researchers are experts on walking, a field that is especially relevant to the question of bigfoots.

According to John Napier, a former director of the Primate Biology Program at the Smithsonian Institution in Washington, D.C., the creature in the video walks more like a modern human than a

primitive, apelike creature. The stride also seems exaggerated and artificial, like bad acting.

Also, the bigfoot's foot size, height, and stride from the film don't correspond well at all. Tall people have big feet and relatively large strides. But based on analysis performed while watching the video, the animal's feet (at fourteen to fifteen inches) are simply too big for its estimated height of about six-foot-five inches, and its modest gait.

There's another "but" in terms of the film's believability. And it regards precisely that: the bigfoot's buttocks. Humans have ample ones; apes don't. Our ancient ancestors evolved them to house the larger muscles needed for walking, running, sprinting, and crouching . . . basically the strength needed to flee wild animals and stay alive on the wide open grasslands and plains. The bigfoot's noticeable derriere in the film posed a red flag to primate experts.

Roger Patterson's character was seen as questionable, too, since he lived a life largely in show business, had a reputation for being a slick salesman, and ultimately profited handsomely from the sale of his film.

Then there's the ease with which the two men found the creature. Thousands of people have logged weeks, months, and years hunting for the hairy ape. How could Patterson and Gimlin fulfill such a monstrous quest in only a few short days?

And what about Mrs. Bigfoot's over-the-shoulder gaze? If the gesture sounds familiar, it's because it is. William Roe, who swore he'd seen a sasquatch in Canada, described the creature moving exactly that way. Some have argued that this haunting description was almost like a script for the film!

BREAK A LEG, BIGFOOT!

There's another monkey wrench in the works when it comes to the Patterson–Gimlin film: It's reportedly hairy, had a zipper, and was kept in a trunk. . . . You guessed it—a gorilla suit! In 1998, a man named Bob Heironimus announced that he was the one wearing it in the much-viewed, fifty-nine-second film. "I'm telling the truth," he stated in his local Yakima, Washington, newspaper at the time, adding, "I'm tired after thirty-seven years."

But why wait so long to "stomp" forward? Heironimus says that, over time, he grew increasingly frustrated for never being paid for his performance—he was apparently promised a thousand dollars by Patterson—which others had profited from.

Bigfoot believers don't believe Heironimus, and since his confession, they've picked apart every one of his statements. They argue that Heironimus can't be trusted and that he's perpetuating his own fraud.

For now, until the actual gorilla suit emerges, it's just one person's word against another. Of course, if polygraph tests are considered reliable, then Heironimus passed one in 2005 with flying colors.

There are a handful of scientists who dispute the critiques made in this chapter. One was anthropologist Grover Krantz, who considered the film very convincing. He said the size and shape of the creature couldn't be duplicated by a human. "Its anatomical details," he once remarked, "are just too good."

Others agree that the animal's apparent bulging muscles would be too difficult to fake—and that such a sophisticated furry costume would have been hard to produce in the 1960s.

Regardless of all the issues with the film, many Bigfoot believers in the 1960s and 1970s weren't ready to give up the search. They have kept on hunting, to this very day.

CHAPTER FOUR
THE MODERN HUNT

"As long as one keeps searching, the answers will come."
—Joan Baez, an American songwriter and singer

Eyewitness accounts, probably more than any factor, keep the hunt for bigfoot animals alive. Looking wide-eyed and shaken, numerous people have stepped forward, insistent that they've laid eyes on one of these large hairy beasts.

Consider these powerful statements made by witnesses who reported their experiences to the Bigfoot Field Researchers Organization, which bills itself as the largest research organization committed to solving the mysteries surrounding bigfoot creatures.

"WHAT I SAW WAS UNFORGETTABLE AND UNBELIEVABLE..."

Julius Mannix

"I'll be going to the grave with this story..."

Jeanne Hutchinson

Jeanne Hutchinson

"I was scared out of my mind..."

Silvester Furilo

Silvester Furilo

Based on decades of searching and note-taking, this is what Bigfoot believers think they know about the wild, apelike creature—including its habitat, food sources, and physical and social characteristics.

A SHIFTING HOME

Where do bigfoots live? If reported sightings are any indication, then almost everywhere! But when you look at a map of the United States that shows recent alleged sightings, you do see clear trends. The alleged creature prefers sprawling dense forests where it can hunt ample deer and small mammals—such regions as the Pacific Northwest and the Appalachian Mountains of Ohio, Georgia, and Kentucky. Bigfoot hunters say it's similar to how lowland gorillas, for instance, inhabit the leafy, tropical forests of central Africa.

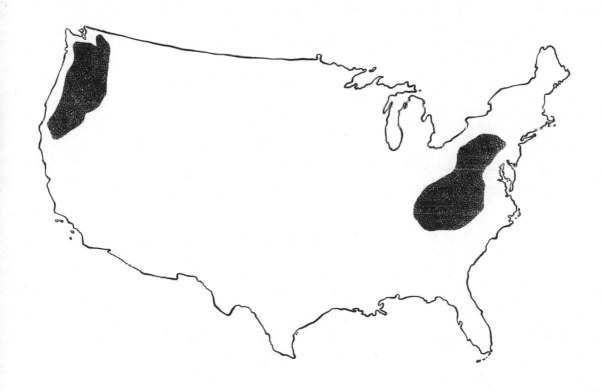

Caves are also said to make prime habitats. They're cool, dark, and generally not frequented by humans. (Who wants to go spelunking for a Sasquatch?!) And according to one 1958 headline from a California newspaper, large underground drainage pipes, or culverts, make perfectly fine beds, too: "Bigfoot Not Fussy, Likes Culverts for His Boudoir"!

A home, by bigfoot standards, is an extensive range. To keep a *low* profile and avoid notice, the eight-foot-plus hairy hiker must always be on the move. It may bed down, or nest, for a short period of time. These beds, made up of bunched-up grasses or other soft vegetation, are pretty cozy—at least that's according to prominent Bigfoot hunter Matt Moneymaker, who says he took a short nap in one!

SASQUATCH SNACKS

Most bigfoots weigh between five hundred and a thousand pounds. Hefty as a grizzly bear, the creature requires a *lot* of food to survive. Fortunately, the animals are said to have a wide-ranging appetite—crunching and munching on everything from leaves, berries, insects, and fish to poultry, deer, elk, and roadkill. When trackers try to bait a bigfoot to learn more about it, they leave out big platters of its favorite treats, which, based on trial and error, they think include apples, bacon, peanut butter, doughnuts, and candy bars. Oh, and raw liver, too.

PEANUT BUTTER

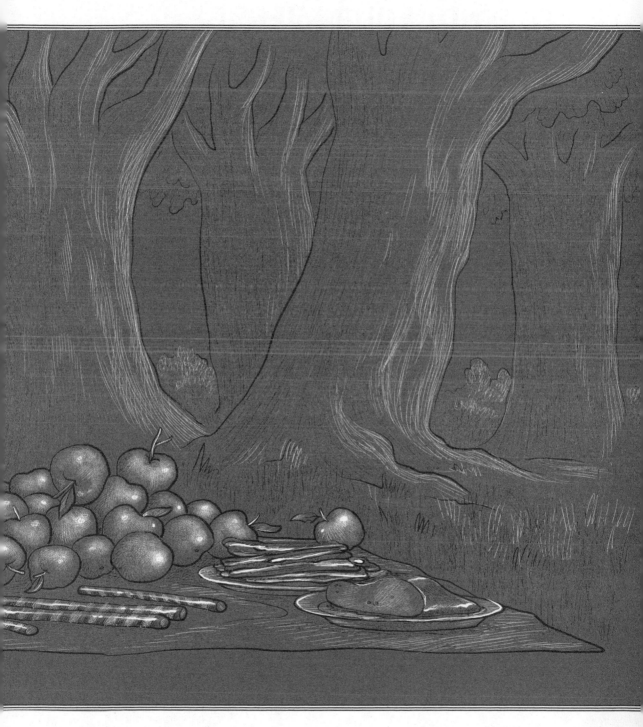

NOT YOUR AVERAGE SASQUATCH

So what do bigfoots look like? It depends on who you ask. Physical descriptions of the creature vary greatly. But, if we're speaking in averages, the animal is said to be about eight feet tall (the height of most ceilings), with long swinging arms, and a thick, short neck. It's covered with dark, humanlike hair, which is different from fur. Fur has two layers and comprises the coats on dogs, cats, and other mammals.

Usually the strong, silent type, bigfoots can also sometimes make a ruckus. The creatures have been known to howl, whoop, and whistle. But according to trackers, they're much less boorish than you might think. Bigfoot hunters say that the reason we find so little evidence of bigfoot activity is that the animal is quite clean and tidy— a good strategy for eluding potential predators!

Bigfoots, however, do possess a few unsavory qualities. The most offensive attribute is probably their smell, which, according to some witnesses, arrives on the trail long before they do. The animal's stench has been compared to feces, rotting meat, and roadkill. (Gag!) And while most reports describe a bigfoot as being docile, there are accounts of the hairy intruder rummaging through garbage cans, stealing produce from gardens, and terrorizing small pets.

NOT A WASTE

And, yes, you've probably been wondering . . . just how big are a bigfoot's, well, droppings? No surprise, the creature's scat—the term scientists use for animal feces—are presumably LARGE. While no scat sample has ever been definitively tied back to Bigfoot, such a poopy find could potentially supply a lot of helpful information, most notably what the creature is hunting and eating.

TOOLS FOR TRACKING

Today's bigfoot hunters have a plethora of nifty tools at their disposal. With music players, they can make sounds that will attract the creature. Video cameras can be stationed throughout the woods to record unusual nighttime activity. Glow-in-the-dark powder can be sprinkled near bait stations with the hopes that a bigfoot will step in it and leave behind glowing footprints in the twilight.

Hi-tech, expensive missions have employed drones outfitted with cameras. Thermal imagers have been used during cold and dark nighttime expeditions. (The screen would definitely turn bright-red if, say, an eight-hundred-pound warm body was nearby!)

The images that have garnered the most excitement and scrutiny in recent times are probably the Jacobs Photographs. In 2007, these black-and-white images were captured in Pennsylvania's Allegheny National Forest one night with a hi-tech trail camera. Using a motion sensor and infrared light, the camera nabbed some sort of hairy animal bent over on the ground. Was it a bear or a bigfoot? Almost a decade later, the question is still being debated!

EYES ALL AGLOW

It's eerie, but it's also ultra-cool: At night, trackers say, a bigfoot's eyes will glow. A variety of mammals possess this feature, especially nocturnal ones such as cats and raccoons. When light shines in these animals' eyes at night, their pupils glow and often assume a spooky red, green, or gold iridescence.

Night creatures evolved this helpful feature so they could exploit precious light sources in the dark. Their eyes contain a special mirrorlike membrane that not only receives light, like our own eyes do, but also reflects it. This allows more light to flood the eye, both as it enters and exits—giving the animal more light to see with. (Want to impress your friends? This special membrane is known as a "tapetum lucidum," which means "bright tapestry" in Latin.)

Even if you don't find a bigfoot, try this nighttime naturalist trick at home: Point a flashlight toward a forest floor, tall grasses, or brush. Are any eyes glowing back at you? These are probably spiders, which also have reflective retinas to help them hunt at night!

CHAPTER FIVE

OUT OF THE WOODS

"Now is the time to understand more, so that we may fear less."
—Marie Curie, a Polish-born French physicist who was the
first woman to be awarded a Nobel Prize

We've done a lot of dodging in this Bigfoot book so far. We all crave clear, concise information. As humans, we seek the truth. (Is it any surprise that *Homo sapiens* means "wise person"?) So you're probably ready for an answer to the burning bigfoot question: Do these stinky

stompers really exist? What are *your* thoughts on Bigfoot? Do you think there could be any truth to all the legends and eyewitness accounts? In this chapter, we'll shine science's unforgiving light on the big, hairy brute. Here we'll bare the truth—Bigfoot warts and all.

TOO BIG TO MISS

Unfortunately, at this point, given the lack of evidence, there is *very little* chance that any bigfoot or sasquatch creatures exist. For the last sixty years, since the Wallace brothers made Bigfoot famous in Bluff Creek, California, numerous scientists have examined the question of a possible wild man/woman. Real experts, with advanced degrees and training in anthropology, biology, ecology, and other relevant disciplines, have pored over the data and supposed evidence.

In all this time, they argue a bigfoot, dead or alive or even in fragments, has not turned up. And in an era when high-resolution cameras seem to be everywhere, we still don't have any verifiable video recording of a hairy, apelike beast.

The critics have other bones to pick with the Bigfoot hypothesis. (By the way, a hypothesis is an idea or possible explanation about something in the world that has not yet been proven.) Here's what they have to say:

BIGFOOT IS FLAKY

One of the problems with bigfoot, researchers say, is the wide-ranging physical descriptions of the animal. Sure, it's normal to see some differences in people's reports, for instance, in the creature's hair color, height, or weight. But the descriptions seem to run the gamut of beastly possibilities.

A bigfoot might have brown, black, white, or red hair. It's been said to have rounded as well as pointed ears. It may be pinheaded or flat-headed. (One observer compared its head shape to the back of Darth Vader's helmet, and his fingers to Snickers candy bars!)

And then there's the issue of the bigfoot's many alleged talents. Some swear that the creature speaks human languages. (Ciao, Sasquatch!) Others claim it disappears—*poof!*—at will, appears in connection with UFOs, *and* has psychic powers (or is able to communicate with humans without even speaking)!

Is it realistically possible to find such diverse physical variation in a single species? According to the vast majority of scientists: no.

BIGFOOT . . . IN STORES NEAR YOU

So you're coming up short in your search for a bigfoot? If you don't mind settling a bit—for a tamer, quieter, less smelly version of the brawny beast, that is—then you need look no further than your local store or online shopping website to find the hairy hiker.

Yes, Bigfoot with a capital "B," while scarce in nature, is easy to spot in American pop culture! And his capacity to make big bucks has proven irresistible to an array of industries. From television to movies (Have you seen *Harry and the Hendersons*?) to musicals (Bigfoot belts it out in *Sasquatched! The Musical*), Bigfoot has left his mark—and continues to do so. The eight-footer was also once a mascot for a former NBA team, the Seattle SuperSonics, and a macho monster truck also carries his name.

Of course, plenty of kitschy consumer goods bear his grungy likeness, too: T-shirts, baseball caps, lunch boxes, toys, and stuffed animals. But first-aid bandages and Bundt cake forms?

Yep, believe it or not, some of the most unexpected products also feature the big guy, including slippers, car fresheners, golf balls, tree ornaments, shaving cream, mints, beef jerky, and even shower curtains!

And what about Bigfoot's true persona? Across pop culture and in the media, he's often depicted as a ruthless killer; other times as a gentle giant. What do you think?

DEFEETED

A lot has been made of bigfoot tracks—large fourteen- and fifteen-inch imprints that would make us shudder if we ever saw them in the woods. Such deep impressions, usually presented to scientists as plaster casts, are offered up as hard, indisputable proof that bigfoots exist.

But it's not that simple. The problem of variation rears its ugly head again. Most of the bigfoot tracks supposedly found have five toes.

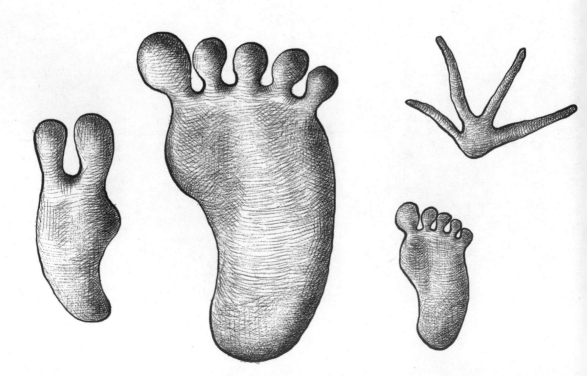

However, some of the casts brought forward by sasquatch seekers show feet with anywhere from two to six toes! The length and width of the feet vary wildly, too. Alleged tracks found by bigfoot hunters have been as ridiculously small as four inches (That's just pathetic, Bigfoot!) to as big as twenty-seven inches! And the tracks' width has reportedly ranged anywhere from three to thirteen inches!

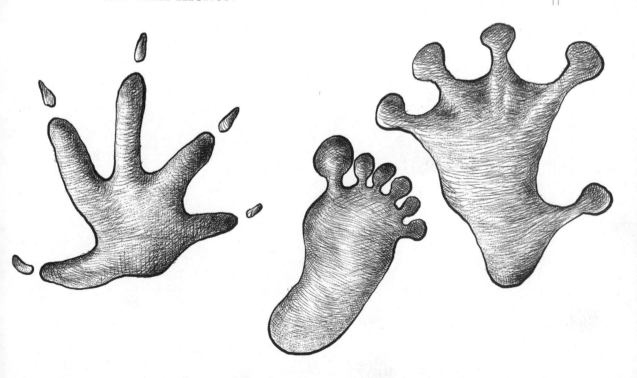

Some investigators try to qualify the data. For example, they might argue that it's more likely that bigfoots have five toes, so research should dismiss any reports stating that the creature has, say, two toes. But what is such a rationale based upon? What's desperately missing, scientists say, is a "type specimen," a dead or alive bigfoot representative that can be used for comparison.

WANTED
BIGFOOT: DEAD OR ALIVE

REWARD:
SINCERE THANKS FROM THE SCIENTIFIC COMMUNITY

MAN . . . URGHH, BEAST . . . IN THE MIRROR

Physical proof is what's ultimately missing in this exhaustive hunt for bigfoot-like beasts. There have been thousands of supposed sightings, glimpses, audio clips, and more. But still, after all this time, no *real*, *actual* creature has been trapped, captured, or clearly caught on a quality film.

That doesn't mean bigfoot is a bust. Not at all. The big legend, as well as our big-hearted love for it, has a lot to teach us. It reminds us of the power of dreams and the imagination. It also reminds us that as humans, we need our stories and myths—apparently as much as we need our opposable thumbs.

WE ARE FAMILY

If the bigfoot exists, you might wonder, would *we* be its relatives? Chances are, yes.

Humans belong to the *Hominidae* family in the organizational system that categorizes all living things. We share this family with the "great apes," which include chimpanzees, gorillas, and orangutans. Among other things, we share a large amount of DNA with these creatures, and we all have a capacity for language. If bigfoots exist, based on all the accounts of their features, they would likely be classified with the hominids, too.

Note: Humans are the only living creatures to be classified in the genus *Homo* and the species *sapiens*! Close relatives of ours include the now-extinct Neanderthals (*Homo sapiens neanderthalensis*), stocky hunters with bulging brows and foreheads who died out around forty thousand years ago!

CONCLUSION

BFF: BIG FOOT FOREVER

"You were once wild here. Don't let them tame you."
—Isadora Duncan, the "Mother of Modern Dance"

I f it's true that bigfoots do not exist in nature, it doesn't mean we can't have our own Bigfoot in spirit.

The idea of a wild wonder prowling out in the woods is fascinating. And the truth is, there are plenty of existing and exciting natural marvels out there to discover.

You can organize your *own* expedition into the forest, woods, or a nearby park. (Ask your parents first, of course!) You can even call it a "Bigfoot Hunt" if you want. Pack up some naturalist essentials—like a notebook and pencil, magnifying glass, tweezers, clear plastic bags, and track-making kit—and take off.

You will undoubtedly find some curiosities and wonders—even if it isn't a whopping fifteen-inch-long footprint!

Main Sources

Blu Buhs, Joshua. *Bigfoot: The Life and Times of a Legend*. Chicago: The University of Chicago Press, 2009.

Brockenbrough, Martha. *Finding Bigfoot: Everything You Need to Know*. New York: Feiwel and Friends, 2013.

Loxton, Daniel and Donald R. Prothero. *Abominable Science! Origins of the Yeti, Nessie, and Other Famous Cryptids*. New York: Columbia University Press, 2013.

Napier, John. *Bigfoot: The Yeti and Sasquatch in Myth and Reality*. New York: E. P. Dutton & Company, 1973.

FOR FURTHER READING

So you keep coming up short in your hunt for Bigfoot, but aren't quite ready to give up the quest? If you don't mind using your imagination, there's a lot more you can read about Bigfoot.

Check out these sources:

The Bigfoot Paradox, by Rebecca Goyte

Bigfoot: Magic, Myth, and Mystery, by Virginia Loh-Hagan

The Bigfoot Field Researchers Organization at: www.bfro.net

Smithsonian National Museum of Natural History website: "What does it mean to be human?" at: www.humanorigins.si.edu